IT'S NOT ALL

JUST JUNK

How to Maximise Your Yard Sale Profits

By Richard Macdonald & Dixie Carlton

ISBN: 978-0-9943838-0-8

Published by Maria Carlton Pty Ltd
Queensland, Australia
www.mariacarlton.com

CONTENTS

INTRODUCTION

'OLD $5 VASE SELLS FOR $5000'

It's a dream for most old collectors to find a 'missing Picasso' or Ming vase in a yard sale or grandma's attic, and while this has been known to happen, a surprising number of people don't know if they have a collectable *anything* worth a few dollars or a few hundred or more.   But when you are contemplating selling something old there are a number of things you can do to help identify and value the items you have.

Hi I'm Richard Macdonald and I've made millions of dollars over the last 30 years buying and selling antiques and collectable items. Frequently I'm asked about how to know if something is worth a lot of money or just junk and I wrote this book to help people in the situation of either:

- a) Clearing out 'mum's old house'.
- b) A marriage breakup and in need of disposing of unwanted jewellery.
- c) Finally sorting out 'all that junk' at home.
- d) Need a bit of spare cash.

Knowing how to pull together the best items for a yard sale, vs what to keep and sell on E-Bay is a real dilemma for many people and if you are in that situation, please know that you're not alone. The pages you are about to read will help you to not only maximise your profits at a yard sale, but also to identify and discover buried treasure at someone else's yard sale – someone not yet smart enough to read this book before inviting people to buy their old stuff.

We wish you happiness and profitability in your future treasure seeking and selling...

CHAPTER 1

RESEARCHING AND ASSESSING VALUE

Put out the most stuff you have - Don't expect to sell all of it, but the more you have the more you'll sell.

Anything you haven't used in the last two years – Walmart/KMart style low cost stuff, and things you've been keeping because 'one day it will come in handy'.

HOW TO GET A GOOD PRICE FOR THE BEST THINGS.
Here's how to understand what things you have among your stuff are the premium items.

Start by putting everything you have into one room. You might have anything from old furniture and clothing, to collector cards, old pottery, porcelain, or crystal from your Grandma, canvas art, jewellery, war souvenirs, or stamps and coins. Collect it all together in one place first.

Some items will be easy to value and will take you only a few minutes. If you don't have the time or inclination to do some very basic research however, I recommend you put this book down right now, and forget about maximising any value from selling your old junk.

Some items will be extremely easy to identify and value on the internet.

TO START WITH – CHECK THE FOLLOWING:

- Coins – the year and country
- Stamps – the year and the pictures
- China/porcelain – the name on the bottom (note – if it says made in China or Taiwan[1] forget about it being of high value, move on to the next item in your pile).
- Silver or Gold – look for the stamped markings, you may need a magnifying glass. (Refer to chapters 11 and 15 respectively.)

Start with E-bay or Gumtree, and find anything similar or the same. If it's nearly exactly the same, then check the quality compared to yours. Then review the price it sold for. The current market value is what the last identical items SOLD for. To identify this look at the Completed Listings to the left of the EBay Screen.

If you are able to identify who the under-bidders were on the last sale, ask if they want to buy your item for that price. You can also price it for your yard sale at that level, knowing you have the potential to sell it for the 'close to' price on E-bay to fall back on.

Consider E-Bay as your back up option but use it to research the interest in your own items.

If there are a lot of the same items on E-Bay, then be prepared to drop the price for a quick sale. If there are very few, or no current/recent items on E-Bay like yours, then be prepared to do some additional research via Google.

---

[1] That's not to say they aren't great collectables from Taiwan and/or China but they predate the 'Made in China' period.

CHAPTER 2

ADDITIONAL RESEARCH OPTIONS:

Visit some local antique stores, talk to dealers of estate or second hand items, and then see if you can get some interest from them in purchasing your item. However, be prepared for the fact that they will not offer you the same price you may have seen listed on E-Bay. They are likely to offer ½ or ¼ of their retail price. The reason for this, is that they have to consider the items may not sell immediately so therefore they will have to carry the stock. They may also need to advertise it to sell it, and they still need to make some profit. This is their business. However, there are some things you need to know about working with a dealer.

See the Antique Dealer as your back up option if the item does not sell via your direct options, such as a yard sale. A good tactic is to have done some research before you talk to a dealer (ie on E-Bay) to have some realistic expectation of value of your item. A good dealer will offer you a price that is as good today as it will be in a week or two. Therefore you can expect that if you don't sell your item directly, you can still go back to him or her and secure the deal after your yard sale.

If you are talking with a dealer who says his buy price is only good for 'right here, right now' then go and find another dealer. This one is only trying to exploit your lack of knowledge and desperation for a sale/money – walk away fast.

RICHARD'S TOP 11 BUYING TIPS:
To help you NOT get ripped off buying second hand or estate items

When entering any second hand or antiques business – whether it's a pop-up store, antique fair, or solid bricks and mortar established business – it's important to know the following things to help ensure you're dealing with legitimate and knowledgeable traders. This is after all an easy business to get hoodwinked in.

1) Are they legitimate and established... Not just new in town with no history.
2) Does the person you are dealing with have any specialist knowledge?
3) Is he or she able to refer you to others in their business community with extra specialised knowledge? This is a sign of their own standing among their peers and associates.
4) Are they a LICENSED Second Hand Dealer? (Able to produce their license easily)
5) Are they and/or their staff respectful, and courteous in their dealings with you?
6) Will they offer a warranty or any guarantees on what they sell?
7) If they offer a discount, does it still reflect a fair profit margin for them? If not, why are they trying to sell it too cheap – this could be a red flag for stolen items, or their heading towards going out of business?
8) Do they have a broad stock base? This means their pricing is most likely good, and they can offer comparative prices for your peace of mind. It's not just 'guesswork' for them.
9) Is their stock clean, and well presented?
10) Are they willing to be patient and not rush you to make a decision about the purchase?

11) Has a friend done prior business with this person and have an opinion?

There are many very good and legitimate second hand dealers, antique and estate specialists around. Most have made a living for a number of years, or in some cases their entire adult lives, buying and selling old treasures. They study their products, and are willing to share their knowledge openly. They also love to learn new things about old things. Many enjoyable conversations can be had with these people. But being cautious when buying from traders of second hand items and antiques is always good business sense. ___

I'd like to emphasise that in my experience most Antique and Second Hand Dealers are good people, and good business operators. 80% of their business is based on repeat and referral, so they have to be honest and reliable in their dealings with customers at both the buying and selling stage.

If you are offered 10-20% below your expected E-Bay price, then I recommend you take it.

CHAPTER 3

YOUR YARD SALE STRATEGY

When you have worked out the value of your items, assuming everything will be sold at your Yard Sale, then you can start pricing your items for sale.

First section them into three categories:

1. Clothing
2. Furniture
3. Knick Knacks or Tools

All of the high value items should be priced at 20% above what you hope to get for it – remembering that everyone who turns up on the day will want to negotiate a bargain with you. This way you can give a little and still get close to your hoped for prices.

Note of Advice on accepting an Offer: If I was offered 50% of what I'd see on E-Bay for anything I was selling, I'd take that offer. Otherwise you can still end up getting stuck with it. Again, review completed listings of similar products before your sale day so that you can ensure your expectations are realistic when it comes to bargaining on a deal.

Furniture is the one thing that is really hard to sell and worth focusing on getting rid of. Apart from book cases, or very unusual (collectable) furniture, always price these to sell and be prepared to let them go. You must be clear on your intention to sell Furniture and therefore you can afford to be least adventurous with your pricing on these items.

My philosophy is to do your best to sell it. You may have a $100 price tag on that table, but be willing to take $30 for it unless you have room to store it for an indefinite period of time.

"If you really want to sell it – then Sell it!"

Another point on pricing to sell furniture. An oak bookcase from the 1930s has a better chance of getting $200 (or above) then if it was an old 1990s clapboard bookcase worth $10.

Timing is everything. In most locations you'll get 50% of your cash from the buyers in the first hour. These are the professional or amateur dealers who know what they are looking for, and are experienced at buying and on-selling. They are always the best to sell to as they just want the margin and will make quick decisions based on experience, not just 'ooh it's pretty'. Later in the day buyers will be looking for cheap home items and tend to be a lot fussier.

CHAPTER 4

CLOTHING

Sometimes there's a market for clothing, however it's not high priced or very lucrative product. For example, even your grandmother's fur stole or mother's debutante gown will struggle to make $50, and that's if they are very good quality. Unless it's truly spectacular, such as a vintage *Oscar de la Renta* gown worn to the Oscars by Grace Kelly – in which case it should be sent to auction anyway – you are likely to struggle to meet your expectations on selling clothing.

Everything will need to be clean, pressed if possible, and priced well below the $50 mark. Think $5-$20 in most instances. Your old children's clothes (and generally items for under three year olds are better sellers) need to be on a $2 table. A bail of old nappies (in excellent condition) are likely to sell at no more than $1.00 each. An old damask Irish linen table cloth that was 'mums' wedding present' might fetch $20-30.

However, Grandma's excellent condition Louis Vuitton handbag or luggage, or Grandad's Gucci driving gloves should be sent to auction.

A note about fur coats. If you have a fur coat with the original owner's name embroidered inside the lining, this is a sign of the highest quality coat. These coats are worth a lot more than one missing this particular detail.

Either way, do your research well before selling a fur coat. Know what the fur is, approximate age, and where purchased from if possible. The sale of furs is a trend that has regained momentum following the downturn in the 1990s, so it's worth taking some time if you have a particularly nice piece.

CHAPTER 5

KNICK KNACKS AND TOOLS

Most KKs if you haven't sent them to be appraised by an expert must be priced to sell.

When it comes to glass ware and crockery, average crystal glasses are worth about $1.00 each, and only sell sets of 4 or 6. If you have 5, then throw the 5th one away. All plates are worth only about 20cent each, or if particularly pretty, you might stretch to $1 each.

The bottom line is to clear the stuff out of your spare room, but make enough money to make it worth your while if you can.

It's important to know that you'll have made 75% of your money on the day by 9am. And that will be on only 25% of your stuff. If you are serious about clearing the rest, then think about what's in the head of your buyer. Unlike the first wave of people to come through early in the morning, these buyers are probably buying for pleasure not for profitable resale. And they don't want to spend too much – it's all based on impulse. They either love something, or don't really care. If they show any interest in something at all, then make sure you don't miss a chance to get rid of it. By this time of the day I'm generally willing to drop my prices by 75% and make sure that interested parties really do walk away with the items left over from the first wave.

If you have any particularly interesting or hi- value items, stand your ground on the prices you expect to get for these especially if you have already secured a backup option from an antique or second hand dealer, or are confident of a sale on E-Bay.

CHAPTER 6

ADVERTISING OPTIONS FOR YOUR YARD SALE

You might like to advertise your yard[2] sale and/or the special items for sale specifically on Facebook and Twitter as well as putting up signs in the street and outside your house.

Facebook is a great way to get the word out there, but it's usually not going to attract people who live in your area.   Mostly you'll end up telling the people you know who live miles away from your place, and missing out on alerting the neighbours.   Twitter is also restrictive unless you have a very large following of people who live nearby.

One thing you could do easily is set up a simple webpage – make the domain name as easy to remember and identify as possible for anyone driving by without a pen to write it down. Something like VivsYardsale.com or www.davesyardsale.biz. Shoot a short video of your items for sale – post it on your web page along with a list of items you wish to sell. Direct ALL your signage, Facebook and any other advertising you are doing (including local newspaper) and encouraging people to go there. You'll be surprised how many people will preview this and form an opinion about your items from there. Include your phone number only if you want people to call ahead of

---

[2] We've used the term Yard sale, to also include Garage sale - the same rules apply.

the day to enquire. This is a great way to presell items. And you'll be able to track the viewer numbers easily.

Countdown – Checklist to Yard Sale Day (YSD).

- ☐ Assemble all items in a room, ideally the garage
- ☐ Identify anything with potential high value
- ☐ List marks and features for your research project
- ☐ Research completed sales of similar/same items on E-Bay and Gumtree
- ☐ Talk to Antique or Second Hand dealers specialising in those items of potential high value
- ☐ Price up all other items for sale
- ☐ Advertise special items online
- ☐ Advertise the yard sale online and in your local community paper
- ☐ Create signs for the street corner and front yard
- ☐ Lay out all stock to sell
- ☐ Be up and ready at least an hour earlier than your advertised start time for early birds who always turn up ahead of the rest
- ☐ Anything that doesn't sell that you can do a deal with online or with a dealer, separate out from the rest of the non-sold items, send the rest to charity.
- ☐ Order a pizza for lunch and enjoy the rest of your weekend!

CHAPTER 7

JEWELLERY

COSTUME JEWELLERY

Costume Jewellery is classified as anything not made from semi-precious, precious stones, or precious organic products such as Jade, Ivory, Coral, or Pearls, Gold, Silver, or Cameo. Some can be worth a lot – but most is virtually worthless. The exception would be something worn by a high ranking celebrity or it's highly branded such as Chanel, Dior, Louis Vuitton etc.

If you have a piece of jewellery and you're unsure of its value or origin, first grab a magnifying glass. See if you can locate a name on it somewhere, or if it's made in China or Taiwan. Chances are it's a low value item, made in mass quantities in an Asian country.

However, many pieces do have a name, so Google and E-Bay search and see if you can find something the same or very similar. Establishing the provenance of your item (made by, approximate age) is your first priority. Then determine if your piece is in as good, worse or same condition as the other(s).

When checking on E-Bay (or any of the similar online sales companies around the world) it's well worth checking the credentials of the seller (of a similar/same item). Click on their name and confirm their pedigree as either a Professional Seller, Trader, Private Person.

A professional seller will have a different agenda than a back yard trader, and a Private Person might be anyone from a regular person who just happens to have something valuable in their cupboard and thought to try selling it, or they might just as easily be an ex-partner trying to get some extra cash from selling an old present or something left behind. A professional seller will have done a lot more homework on the value of something than 'Betty with a Grudge' will have.

Check on the 'completed sales' listings as pro-sellers will have 1000+ sales and will be serious about selling, and priced items accordingly. Whereas someone with only 36 sales means he or she is inexperienced and not as reliable for gauging a price by.

REAL VS FAKE JEWELLERY

To identify if your jewellery is 'real' vs fake or a good copy, read the relevant chapters in this book. If you are still unsure, then seek the advice of a jeweller, licensed valuer, or specialist antique dealer. But the following information will help you in most instances before you need to seek professional help. As for the value of any item please refer to the advice specified already about researching online for similar items as a starting point.

THE DOWNSIDE OF COLLECTING ESTATE JEWELLERY

The downside of collecting and wearing estate jewellery however is finding the right size of something. It's no secret that as a race, human beings have increased markedly in size over the last 100 years as our diets and state of general health and well-being have improved. So it's no surprise really that bangles, bracelets, and rings can often be too small for modern fingers and wrists. Don't despair if you find a beautiful piece that you love, as resizing or repurposing antique items is relatively easy in most cases. Repurposing might mean turning a bold ring setting into a stunning pendant or brooch, or *vis a versa*. Some beautiful rings can be made by highly creative and artistic jewellers using valuable stones.

Bespoke jewellery items are expensive, and if you don't want something that was featured on the front page of a modern jeweller's catalogue then consider gracing your lovely hands or neck with something old, unique, and finely crafted by artisans of merit from a century or two ago.

CHAPTER 8

PEARLS

For more than 2000 years Pearls have been used as a symbol of love, success, social rank, and have therefore been used to enhance many royal crowns - including most English ones - for centuries. They have long been associated with purity and beauty, and although they fell out of favour for a while during the early part of last century, they are now firmly back in fashion. However the fashions of pearls has stepped aside from the traditional styles and more common now are the freshwater and baroque styles despite or perhaps because of their imperfect nature. That's not to say there is not a huge appreciation of and associated high value still placed on traditional pearls.

Cultured and natural pearls start their life when an irritant, either a grain of sand or a placed seed pearl finds its way into a live oyster, mussel, or similar mollusc. As a natural pearl (the irritant is usually naturally placed there and not by means of human interference) there is higher value placed on them. The recipient oyster will try to reject the irritant and in so doing produces nacre, which hardens and builds up in layers resulting in the pearl finish. The final lustre of the Nacre (pronounced NAYkur) determines the shine of the pearl and therefore the final value. It's impossible to overstate how important the finish is to the value of both natural and cultured pearls.

PEARLS FOR KINGS AND SULTANS

Natural pearls are extremely rare and historically have been found in most abundance outside the Pacific in the Persian Gulf. Through trade and plunder they often found their way into the crowns of royalty around the world, turbans of India, and notably the crown of Elizabeth 1 of England. Back in the days of medieval Europe pearls were high on the list of most desired evidence of wealth and inspired an unquenchable appetite for them.

Through later years the art of creating pearls through the 'cultured' pearl process as described above and the Japanese excelled at the craft. The first Akoya pearls were cultured in the early 1920s and is it said their white colour and rose overtone greatly complimented a fair complexion. Akoya pearls are regarded as the highest standard of cultured pearl and one name stands out above all others in this industry - and that name is Mikimoto.

Any set of pearls - from an antique collectors point of view - needs to be well matched in size, with solid gold clasps (or earring posts) and often with Mikimoto Pearls in particular, you will generally find a deeper and more beautiful lustre, with very few blemishes.

One thing that adds to the value of any set of pearls, and the high quality ones in particular, is that over 10,000 individual pearls may be sorted before a 16" single strand of beautifully matched pearls is assembled. Therefore even cultured pearls of high quality can be very expensive.

RESTRINGING PEARLS

My advice if your pearls need to be restrung is to use a re-stringer who only works with natural silk and who only places a single knot between each pearl. It is my personal opinion that double-knotting takes from the look of pearls and casts the eye to the knots more than to the actual pearl. It's also important to consider how the string is inevitably attached to the clasp. If it is simply knotted to a metal clasp your chance of wear and tear and eventual breakage is increased significantly. I personally insist all of our pearl strands are 'gimped'. Gimping is where the re-stringer will use a flexible beading wire that the string can run through at the point it joins the clasp, so protecting it from wear. This attention to detail is the sign of a high quality re-stringer at work, vs a shoddy back yard worker. When it comes to pearls, it's best to pay for the better quality option to preserve their value in the long term.

CARE OF PEARLS

Pearls will take on a dull yellowish brown appearance if they are allowed to contact perfumes, hair sprays and excessive perspiration etc. There is a saying, that pearls are the last thing on, on your way out, and the first thing off, when you arrive home.

As pearls may dry out and crack with time they should be cleaned with a moist soft cloth from time to time. When caring for your pearls it is best not to wet the string or cord, as it may rot over time. The pearl itself is better off in water than air!

If you wear your pearl necklace or bracelet frequently then restringing is advisable every year or two, both from the security viewpoint, and a dirty brown string does nothing to enhance the beauty of your pearls.

To identify whether your pearls may be of reasonable value or not, first look at the stringing of them. A reasonable or high quality strand of pearls will be knotted between every pearl. And the clasp will be of high quality if they are 'real' cultured or natural pearls. These are relative to the value of each strand. Also the colour, and how much nacre remains on a very old set of pearls will help determine current value.

CHAPTER 9

CAMEOS, JADE, BONE

CAMEOS

Cameo jewellery is what is commonly referred to as relief images – most often portraits - carved onto a contrasting plain surface such as shell or glass. This is referred to as an 'assembled cameo, although it was also possible to find more complex versions carved onto single stone items with natural shades and textures. In ancient and renaissance times cameos were also carved by a far more difficult, method directly out of banded agate or layered glass, where different layers have different colours.

Cameos were not always used as jewellery and some great sized *objets d'art* cameos dating back hundreds of years are on display in museums around the world.

Napoleon cultivated a renewed trend in Cameo popularity by having his crown decorated with cameos. In Britain, King George III and then his granddaughter Queen Victoria also made them very popular - so much so that they became a hugely popular industry in the latter half of the 19th century. The most common shells used then were conch shell from the Pacific, which are softer than mussel or mollusc shells used previously, but the conch shell does fade over time.

Check the setting of your cameo – whether it's a ring, brooch, earrings or pendant, the gold or silver setting will help to determine the value of it combined with its overall condition and the detail and quality of the image. Black coral is highly valued, and extremely rare. White and red coral are often found in both antique and modern jewellery items. Conservationists and ecologists recommend against coral harvesting due to depletion of sources worldwide, however it is argued by many that Red Coral is not endangered and so the trade in this continues. Most often coral is turned into beads and used in a variety of natural and polished jewellery styles.

BONE
CITS agrees is it permitted as long as it pre-dates 1947. Bone has blood capillaries running through it and close examination will show three things:

1) Absence of Ivory diamond pattern referred to above.
2) Presence of blood flecks – dead and dried blood resting in the capillary channels
3) Sometimes fine channels looking like drilled channels.

Bone enjoys only a very small value compared to ivory.

JADE
Jade is very difficult to value and often confused with crysophase and quartz, however real jade is very valuable. The most common jade is imperial jade from China, which is lighter green than the highly prized 'pounamu' greenstone from New Zealand, and Russian Jade.

IVORY
Ivory is characterised by its purity of whiteness, but you should also see clear lines running through it which created a checked cross-grain effect which is impossible to duplicate and never present in anything except ivory. Ivory has a softness to the touch whereas bone has a clatter.

The sale of modern ivory is illegal worldwide, however old ivory that predates 1947 is still permitted with the exception of some states and countries. The CITES Agreement came into effect in 1989 regarding this.

If you are an owner of Ivory pieces and would prefer to be selling ivory rather than keeping it, please talk with us about your pieces and your feelings on this. Your items may turn out to be very old vs relatively new (ie early 1900s). If you found out your ivory was several hundred or even thousands of years old, would you feel differently about it? Maybe. We'd like to see the cessation of the ivory trade, but also understand that some very old ivory is simply beautiful and highly collectible. Our role in the selling and buying of Ivory is not to perpetuate an industry that is fraught with anxiety and illegal trade, but to honour the past craftsmanship of what was once a time honoured tradition for artists working in this rare and beautiful medium.

CHAPTER 10

MOURNING JEWELLERY

Mourning jewellery was traditionally worn to acknowledge and commemorate the death of a loved one. This has been a tradition for literally hundreds of years and was also present in Egyptian tradition. The 15th Century throughout Europe saw a significant increase and refinement in this jewellery style. Black became *'de riguer'* and this has remained more or less a constant since. In a time of no photography, it was a way to have a precious reminder of that person with you always.

While this wasn't exactly the dark ages, it was still a time when dying was easy. Childbirth, infection, TB, and a hundred other ailments and mishaps which today we can treat in a week, carried off a ridiculous number of people and especially children. In 1890 the infant mortality rate was 150 per 1000, that's 15%. So, this was not an uncommon event. At the same time the rate of women dying in childbirth was sitting at 60 per 1000. While this actually represented one of the 'least' likely ways for women to die, it was particularly tragic because these women and babies were generally fit and healthy then suddenly dead.

Black enamel or Jet is the traditional material of most mourning pieces. However different metals and gems have different meanings. White enamel means the deceased was a woman who died unmarried and a virgin and pearls generally (but not always) would indicate the loss of a child. Black jet was commonly used in the form of brooches to show Mourning, but often for a non-family member.

Possibly the most macabre, and yet enormously popular material is human hair. This would often be braided into a necklace onto which a mourning brooch or pendant would be attached, which in itself may have had some of the deceased person's hair curled up and visible through glass on the back. This was either mounted, curled around, or sometimes intricately braided. In both cases it was mounted on a piece of silk, cut to leave a criss-cross upstanding grain, thus holding the hair perfectly in place.

Men would often have their dearly departed wife's hair plated into a fob 'chain' and wear it on the front of their waistcoat. In fact this is the most common form of human hair jewellery we still find and sell.

Some more uncommon mourning jewellery will feature a picture with a ship. The ship's presence on a ring like this represents the journey into the afterlife, while the beached anchor symbolizes hope for those the loved one left behind.

Queen Victoria, whose epic sadness over the tragic loss of her husband Prince Albert in 1861, popularized the tradition of wearing mourning jewellery in Great Britain. In fact she wore her husband's mourning ring for the rest of her life. I have personally sold many German mourning rings dated in the 1850's immediately predating Prince Albert's death. It is after his death we see a significant upswing in this jewellery type and style coming out of England and Wales. Being mindful of the fact he was himself German, it could be this tradition was given a boost of popularity riding on the coattails of an already popular and well defined German tradition.

Once photographs were introduced to the public, the combination of lockets and mourning jewellery was pretty obvious. Lockets often featured lilies of the valley which was a common flower used in mourning jewellery as they symbolized the tears of the Virgin Mary. A dark coloured enamel locket could signify that it was created for the final stage of mourning when darker colours (like blue, grey and purple) would be integrated back into the wardrobe.

CHAPTER 11

SILVER AND GOLD

Gold and silver have enjoyed record prices per gram at times in the past and consistently so. Gold charms, gold pendants, brooches and rings are commonly collected for their charm as much as for their value by many collectors. Scrap gold is valued by gram and carat - for example, the value of 18ct gold should be exactly double that of 9ct gold.

There is a stamp usually found on all silver and gold items, however sometimes if a ring has been resized, this may be missing. In which case it will need to be tested to see if it's real. Hallmark legislation[3] has also changed over the years and this may also be a reason why a piece is not marked.

---

[3] Prior to 1975 many precious metals were exempted from hallmarking or stamping. Wedding rings were the exception to this rule. If a piece of jewellery was manufactured prior to 1950 the hallmark may be missing but it will still be described and sold as precious metal if the seller can prove it to be of minimum fineness and manufactured prior to 1950.

Plated Gold vs Rolled Gold – this is exactly the same, just a different term. Rolled gold is literally rolled onto a base metal, generally over silver or copper.

Silver – Standard sterling silver is usually stamped at 925 somewhere on the item, or has Hallmarks indicating town and year of manufacture, and who the silversmith was.

Gold – 9ct, 10ct, 12ct, 14ct, 18ct and 22ct are the most common. The lower the number, the less actual gold is included in the metal mix. What many people are unaware of is that 22ct is almost pure gold and very soft. Too soft for anyone but non-workers to wear, so they say. The reality is, that very soft gold might bend or lose shape if knocked about too much. Harder gold is therefore used most commonly for rings, especially wedding and engagement bands, so that they will withstand years of wear and tear.

Gold also comes in Yellow, Rose, and White gold. This is based on the mix of brass, copper, or nickel with the gold.

COMMON GOLD MARKS AND THEIR MEANINGS:
- 9ct = .375 (parts per thousand) = 37.5%
- 10ct = .417 = 41.70%
- 12ct = .500 = 50%
- 14ct[4] = .585 = 58.5%
- 18ct = .750 = 75%
- 22ct = .916 = 91.6%
- 24ct = .990 = 99.95%
- 1 Troy[5] Oz equals 31.03 grams

Pure gold is naturally yellow, however coloured golds are produced by adding alloys such as silver, copper or brass to crate yellow, green, red, and rose golds.

White gold is never more than 18ct (75%) as the manufacturers need to leave 25% of its parts to dilute the natural yellow of gold and produce the

---

[4] It's also uncommon but possible to find 15ct gold (.625) which was legal from 1854-1931.

[5] A 'Troy' ounce relates only to precious metals.

final white metal needed. This is generally achieved by mixing nickel or palladium.

Platinum is a lustrous, ductile, and malleable (easily worked) silver-white precious metal. Pure platinum is harder than pure iron.

CHAINS

Silver is always worth less than gold; currently worth (as at the start of 2016 in Australia) $19 per ounce, but has been up as high as $43 per ounce in early 2011.

Gold is currently worth $1480 per ounce, which is approximately 3x its value in 2004.

To see if your gold or silver chain is plated, hold a magnet over it and see if it picks it up. If it does, it's plated over another metal. Neither gold nor silver are metallic. However this does not mean it's NOT plated. A professional needs to check it.

If your jewellery item is real and you believe it to be of significant value, then we recommend having it professionally valued. This might be an investment starting at $50 by a licensed valuer. However it will give you a much better idea of what you have, what you might expect to need to insure it for, and what you could expect to sell it for. Be advised that your licensed valuation is for insurance purposes, for replacement if stolen or lost. Your likely price to sell your jewellery to a licensed second hand dealer will be between 10 and 20% in most cases unless your item is truly special, rare, or spectacular.

HALLMARKS

A silver item will nearly always boast a tiny mark discreetly on the base of the item called an assayer's mark. The United Kingdom has one of the most rigid hallmarking systems in the world, and you can learn a lot about a silver or gold item from these tiny stamps, aside from just their metal components. In 1697 a 'Britannia Standard' was developed to help prevent sterling silver coins from being melted down to make silver plate. The requirement of *Britannia* Silver is that it has a millesimal fineness of at least 958, be 95.84% pure silver and only 4.16% of copper. Sterling Silver has a millesimal fineness of 925, meaning the silver alloy component is 92.5% silver and only 7.5% copper. Fine Silver has a millesimal fineness of 999. It is considered to be too soft for general use and is mainly used to make bullion bars for commodities trading.

The United States did not adopt an assaying system, although some cities such as Baltimore had its own assay office from 1814-1830. Sterling silver was adopted as the standard of purity in 1868. Companies such as Tiffany and Gorham developed their own date marking system, and American manufacturers did apply a maker's mark. Those old hallmarks were as unique as logos and fiercely defended just as trademarked logos are today.

While the National Gold and Silver Marketing Act still does not require a quality stamp for silver or gold, there is a requirement for a quality mark accompanies by the manufacturers registered hallmark. This is so that any questions that arise regarding the metal content or quality can be asked of the manufacturer directly.

There are many books and research pages on the internet that help identify manufacturers' marks and are well worth looking up if you wish to know more about the origin of your pieces.

COMMON HALLMARKS

The identifying Assayer Office (that tested and confirmed the item):

Birmingham   Edinburgh   London   Sheffield

Traditional Marks:

Gold   Silver (Sterling)   Silver (Britannia)   Platinum   Palladium

Gold Standard Marks:

 375 585 750 916 990 999

(9 carat)   (14 carat)   (18 carat)   (22 carat)

Silver Standard Marks:

800 925 958 999

Sterling   Britannia

41

Commemorative Marks:

Silver Jubilee Coronation Silver Jubilee Millennium Golden Jubilee Diamond Jubilee
1935   1953   1977   1999-2000   2002   2012

Date of Manufacturer Marks:

2011   2012   2013   2014   2015   2016

CHAPTER 12

COLLECTABLES – LET'S TALK CHRISTMAS

People these days collect so many weird and wonderful things that it's almost impossible to discuss them all here so instead of trying to do justice to a wide range of them, instead we'll focus on one particular popular theme; Christmas Treasures.

It may surprise you to know that it was the Americans who first started decorating small trees and wreaths with nuts, candy, and fruits back in the early 1800s. They would then sometimes take their trees outside for the wildlife to enjoy consuming the leftovers. Popcorn was a popular garland to make to go around the trees too. But it wasn't until Victorian times more than 100 years later that Christmas decorations became more elaborate and well thought out around icons and images we know today. German craftsmen famously started producing images of hearts, stars and angles in glass and metal, and FW Woolworth began importing these for his five and dime stores in the late 1880s. This sparked a raging trend over homemade textile and wooden ornaments. Many were made from pressed tin, cardboard and whatever oddments could be found around the house.

After World War 1, the German ornaments trade floundered and was picked up by American manufacturers. By the 1930s it was big business indeed, assisted by the popularity of department stores who got on the marketing wagon with Santa events in their stores for families. Big window and store displays of toys and Christmas ornaments are something we're all used to now, but those early toys and images used and even their marketing posters and signage are highly collectable now.

By the 1950s, Americans began hankering for elaborate baubles and aluminium Christmas trees in all colours – some of which are still highly sought after by collectors.

ICONS AND FIGURINES

Elves, Reindeer, Angles, Christmas bells and Stars have long been traditional ornaments, but in 1892 the Tchaikovsky Nutcracker Suite Ballet introduced Nutcrackers into the line-up. I once visited a four story home converted into a Christmas Store/Museum in *Rothenberg Ob der Tauber, Germany* that boasts a collection of more than 2000 nutcrackers, some dating back nearly 2,000 years. So these were clearly not always a 'Christmas thing' but have become highly collectable as Christmas Associated items over the years.

Images of Santa were made popular in the 1930s by Coca Cola putting him in a red suit and portraying him as a cheerful gift giver – the colour and image has lasted well through the decades and Santa as we know him now has perhaps been one of the most brilliant advertising campaigns by Coca Cola (or any company for that matter) ever undertaken. Hi quality early memorabilia of Santa in Red, holding a bottle of Coca Cola is also highly collectable.

Finally, music is a big part of Christmas and over the years many Christmas songs and special albums have been recorded by everyone from Bing Cosby to Alvin and the Chipmunks. Posters and Original Albums from older days gone by are also highly collectable – some much more than others. Memorabilia from old Christmas movies are also highly prized by some collectors.

CHAPTER 13

PROVENANCE

Provenance is a word you hear a lot in this industry. It's often bandied around by experts on TV shows like Antiques Roadshow and Bargain Hunt for example. Quite simply provenance is the history of something - where it came from, how old it might be, and anything of particular note about something in the antiques and collectables game is worth knowing simply because something truly special with a clear provenance is usually worth a lot more.

For example, we've just purchased (and will sell) a collection of medals given to Charles Arthur Banks CMG, who was the 17th Lieutenant Governor of British Columbia. Born in New Zealand in 1885, he had a colourful and glorious career which included a long history with the Canadian Government. The medals and other memorabilia we have are enhanced in value by our knowing why he was awarded these, a lot about his career, and therefore why he is of particular interest to collectors.

In Banks case, he is of particular interest to the mining industry for having been awarded the Mining and Metallurgical Society of

America's Gold Medal (and yes it's solid gold and weighs more than you'd imagine) for his role in the aerial development of remote mines.

Medals are an interesting thing in this regard. If you have a medal for your grandfather or uncle who was awarded a service medal for the 1st or 2nd World War, that's one thing, but to find there is also a Victoria Cross in the collection, and to find out exactly what the story was behind being given that, it another thing entirely. There are different ways to value such things, and the best way is to talk with an expert on history and in particular military history in the geographical area that relates to where the medals were awarded. We know that the memorabilia relative to Charles Arthur Banks would be of much greater interest to someone living in Canada or British Columbia than someone living in the USA, UK, or even Australia for example.

Another example of knowing the provenance of an item for sale that we purchased and then later sold in early 2016 is a Naval Telescope. Not just any old telescope as it turns out - this one came off the (pre-Dreadnought) HMS Majestic Battleship which was sunk during the assault on Gallipoli in the Dardenelles. We've learned that it was a gift to an Australian Soldier who assisted in the rescue of many of the sailors at Gallipoli, including in this case an officer.

This rare piece of Gallipoli is even more special (and therefore collectible) due to the story behind how it came to be in the possession of the soldier, as well as the fact that it came from a ship that sunk during the battle. This not only increases its value, but also adds to this history of the item as it's tracked through the decades since being installed on the HMS Majestic.

Not only is it great to have the history of any collectible item, but to have the item in excellent condition (despite or due to) its history is another key part of its value.

Whenever possible we try to ensure the provenance of collectible items we sell so that their history can be preserved by the next owners, and that history passed on with the items.

CHAPTER 14

OLD FASHIONED QUALITY AND CRAFTSMANSHIP

These days, most of the jewellery you can buy is cast in moulds, and finished by hand instead of being designed and created from the ground up. There are differences in quality therefore too, as well as the stones used and enhancements employed. It takes a lot more work to do intricate bridging that will last through years of wear and tear. The common trait of using synthetic or enhanced gemstones means the bling seen on many fingers, ears, and necks nowadays is a lot less expensive than their antique contemporaries.

Emeralds are gorgeous green stones and increasingly rare, Tanzanite is no longer mined, but comes in a stunning array of rich colours, and sapphires in pinks, yellows, and greens are worth far more than most of their similarly sized blue and red (ruby) cousins. Diamonds on the other hand are still stockpiled and released into the markets around the world slowly so as to ensure the prices remain high. If you are seeking high quality jewellery, you are likely to find something made to last longer, with more highly prized and rare stones in something older than a jewellery chain store special.

There are some fundamental differences between antique buyers and modern treasure seekers. For one thing, in the past, most jewellery and silverware was hand-made, crafted by artisans who had spent years learning their trade, As many as seven years at the furnaces to become a trained silver or goldsmith in days of old ensured that the intricate craftsmanship was truly worthy of the stamp the finished items bore.

The other thing that treasure seekers are keen to find when shopping for antiques and estate items is history and the stories that go with the items they buy. For example, knowing that the beautiful necklace with Peridot, Amethyst, and Seed Pearl inlays was a feature of the suffragette movement means a lot to some people. Knowing that Jet jewellery was made famous as a 'mourning stone' by Queen Victoria also dates it and makes it mean more to wear (or simply collect) for some. And finding a beautifully carved Cameo worn by a lady in rustling silk skirts at the King's Palace in Edwardian times also makes it a bit extra special for some.

CHAPTER 15

SUMMARY

If you are faced with the prospect of having to clear out your family home and working out what may or may not be of value or interest to someone else, one of the easiest things you can do is contact two or three antique and estate specialists, auctioneers who specialise in house lots, and discuss your situation with them. However, do your homework. Get some ideas of value of some of the things you have, using the research tips suggested.

Most importantly you have to be happy with the prices offered and the suggestions made by professional people in this realm, and your expectations are going to be most easily managed if you have at least some information already in hand about your possessions.

Don't be afraid to ask for a second opinion on prices offered either.

Items of value may or may not diminish over time. Collectables such as stamps and coins are in the unfortunate position of having fewer people wanting to collect them as the population ages. While the internet makes encyclopaedias almost completely redundant, so too the oversupply of (low cost) china and kitchenware means that high value porcelain and silverware become less appealing for homemakers.

Your old junk may be best moved on to the Op Shops and Charity Houses in your area, or you may find some real treasures buried among your 'old junk'.

We wish you well in finding these treasures, and in seeking and trading other people's treasures if that's what you are keen to do. And we also wish for many happy hours of recycling and repurposing of 'old junk' to take place across the planet for the sake of all the landfills and dumpsters everywhere.

ABOUT THE AUTHORS

Richard Macdonald and Dixie Carlton have been best friends for 30+ years (and married for some of that time), with a shared passion for antiques and estate jewellery. Their business – Magpies Antiques & Collectables has been operating in Queensland since 1999, and started with Richard returning to his love of buying and selling 'old junk' from his university days.

A genius for remembering history and information, Richard is a 'walking encyclopaedia' when it comes to some areas of the antiques industry and can regale anyone interested in discussing items such as militaria, coins, and ancient history for hours. His stories are endless, his knowledge deep, and Google is his *very best friend*. If he doesn't know something about an item for sale, he'll research it until satisfied with the results.

Dixie is the business and marketing manager in this team, and they employ three other people who are also intensely curious and appreciative of historical and antique items.

Richard and Dixie live and work just south of Brisbane, Australia.

- www.magpies-collectables.com
- www.facebook.com/MagpiesCollectables

28482851R00033

Printed in Great Britain
by Amazon